THE STORIES OF
THE MONA LISA

For **Maya Barsony**,
and her cousins **Roxanne**, **Shoshana**, **Héloïse**, and **Nora**.

Based on an idea by **Nadine Nieszawer**.

Sky Pony Press books may be purchased in bulk at special discounts for sales promotion, corporate gifts, fund-raising, or educational purposes. Special editions can also be created to specifications. For details, contact the Special Sales Department, Sky Pony Press, 307 West 36th Street, 11th Floor, New York, NY 10018 or info@skyhorsepublishing.com.

Sky Pony® is a registered trademark of Skyhorse Publishing, Inc.®, a Delaware corporation.

Visit our website at www.skyponypress.com.

10 9 8 7 6 5 4 3 2 1

Manufactured in China, June 2012
This product conforms to CPSIA 2008

Library of Congress Cataloging-in-Publication Data

Barsony, Piotr, 1946- author, illustrator.
[Histories de Joconde. English]
The stories of the Mona Lisa : an imaginary museum tale about the history of modern art / Piotr Barsony ; translated from the French by Joanna Oseman.
pages cm
ISBN 978-1-62087-228-4 (hardcover : alk. paper)
1. Painting, Modern--Juvenile literature. 2. Art movements--Juvenile literature. 3. Leonardo, da Vinci, 1452-1519. Mona Lisa--Juvenile literature. I. Oseman, Joanna, translator. II. Barsony, Piotr, 1946- Paris : Hugo & Cie, 2010. Histoires de Joconde Translation of III. Title.
ND190.B2513 2012
759.06--dc23
2012015603

Artistic direction: Sandrine Granon and Stéphanie Aguado
Paintings: Piotr Barsony

THE STORIES OF THE MONA LISA

AN IMAGINARY MUSEUM TALE ABOUT THE HISTORY OF MODERN ART

PIOTR BARSONY

TRANSLATED FROM THE FRENCH BY JOANNA OSEMAN

Sky Pony Press
New York

"Dad, will you tell me a story?"

"A story?"

"Yes, any story you want."

"Okay, sure. Why don't I tell you a story about the history of painting?"

"Painting has its own story?"

"Of course it does. And the *Mona Lisa*, the most beautiful painting in the whole world, is going to guide us through it."

"How come that's the most beautiful painting in the world?"

"Nobody has ever been able to portray as much life in a face as Leonardo da Vinci did with the *Mona Lisa*. And life equals beauty."

"It looks like a photo . . ."

"At the time, before photography had been invented, portraits had to be as accurate and realistic as possible. If I were to order a portrait of my daughter, for example, I would expect expect to see my daughter on the canvas."

"So, when photos were invented, all the painters lost their jobs?"

"No, they just changed how they went about their work. The desire for paintings that looked like their subjects meant that accuracy and delicate shading and coloring were vital, but these requirements were suddenly no longer necessary. You could say that everything a photo did, the painters stopped doing by themselves."

"So, what did they do?"

"That's what I'm going to tell you about."

"You can't see this Mona Lisa very well. It's just her reflection."

"This is a painting by Claude Monet. It dates from 1875 and is called *Impression, Sunrise*."

"I prefer the Leonardo da Vinci one."

"That's fine, but you're going to have to learn how to look at things differently."

"How?"

"You'll see. Here, everything is just color and light. Monet didn't worry about likeness, but rather about the impression of likeness. If you look again, the drawing seems to have vanished."

"Ah-ha! That's why he called it *Impression, Sunrise*!"

"Exactly. And this is the painting that gave its name to the great painting movement called Impressionism. The Impressionists' first exhibition took place in the studio of a photographer named Nadar."

"Weren't they angry with the photographers?"

"No, the invention of photography was like a liberation for painters, an

opportunity to explore new things."

"Why did he give the same name to two of his paintings?"

"Look carefully, silly! It's not the same artist. The other painting is by an Englishman named William Turner and was painted four years earlier."

"So, Monet copied him?"

"Monet saw a Turner exhibition in London, and it obviously inspired him greatly. In fact, you could say that William Turner was the first of the Impressionists. And Impressionism is . . .?"

"Color and light."

"Good job! The day that Monet died, one of his friends, Georges Clemenceau—who was also a French politician—cried out: 'No black for Monet!' Then he ripped down the colorful curtains that were in the bedroom where the body was resting and used them to cover his friend. So, as you see, 'color and light' is a philosophy that extends even beyond death."

William Turner

VAN GOGH

"She looks pretty against the blue sky!"

"This is *Starry Night* by Vincent Van Gogh, a Dutch painter who lived in France."

"It looks like it's made up of waves . . ."

"Van Gogh put his troubles and torments onto the canvas."

"Is that how he saw the *Mona Lisa*?"

"We see just as much with our hearts as we do with our eyes."

"Why did he paint if he was so sad?"

"Because painting made him feel better and less anxious, took him away from his 'black moments,' as he used to say."

"Ah-ha! He put suns in the sky to make everything better!"

"Without a doubt. He also painted sunflowers, plants that look like the sun and are always pointing towards its rays. The strange thing is that his self-portraits are done in the same reds and yellows as his sunflowers."

"Did he want to be a sunflower?"

"I'm not sure he wanted to really be one. But just like them, he was always looking for the best possible light. That's why he moved to Arles, which is a very sunny town in the south of France. He was obsessed with light, both exterior and interior. As a young man, he wanted to be a pastor so that he could preach about spiritual light to the men who worked overnight in the coal mines of Northern France."

"Was he an Impressionist, like Monet?"

"At that time almost everyone was. The difference was that Monet painted what he could see, whereas Van Gogh painted what he felt inside. You could say that he was expressing his own impressions."

Paul Gauguin

"Wow, this Mona Lisa is beautiful! Such nice colors!"

"This is by Paul Gauguin. As you can see, Gauguin's work is all about color. When he added some red, he would say, 'This is the most beautiful red in the world.'"

"What about green?"

"The most beautiful green in the world, of course! This Mona Lisa was painted in Tahiti. She looks a bit like a statue, because Gaugin was strongly influenced by Polynesian sculpture. It was a way for him to escape the influences of the West."

"He traveled a long way away to paint!"

"Because he could. The paint tube had just been invented, making it a lot easier for artists to travel. Before, they had too many materials to carry with them: paint pots, varnish, binders, fixatives, and so on. With a tube, everything is in the same place."

"Did Gauguin like light too, like Van Gogh?"

"Of course. They were very good friends actually, but they used to fight a lot."

"Well, that makes sense. One of them did flat paintings; the other used lots of waves."

"They must have had very different personalities."

"Were there other Impressionist painters?"

"Yes, a lot."

"Why aren't we going to look at them?"

"I can't tell you about everything; it would take too long! We have to choose carefully. After that it's up to you to find out whatever you want on your own."

12   IMPRESSIONISM—PAUL CÉZANNE (1839-1906)

"This one is Paul Cézanne's *Mona Lisa*. Now pay attention. This is going to be a tricky one."

"It looks like the others to me, just with fewer colors."

"Paul Cézanne was trying to resolve a problem. How do you get depth without the usual techniques of perspective, shading, and color tones? To get this depth, he decided to look at nature in terms of shapes and to put the colors next to each other without blending them together. Look at this Mona Lisa. The background is made up of little green squares and between them, there is a small space. The colors aren't blended together like with Monet."

"I think I understand . . ."

"To get a better sense of how he painted, you should go to your computer and look up his Mont Sainte-Victoire series. It will be much easier to see it there than on a portrait because there are lots of different planes."

"Was he an Impressionist?"

"In the sense that he only used color, yes he was. But, unlike the others, he didn't use it as a source of color vibration or of light. He used it for the composition and construction of his different planes."

"It's complicated!"

"I told you it would be; it's unusual. You could say that Cézanne was a kind of researcher."

"A researcher?"

"Yes, because he tried to apply a method and a theory to his work. That's why it was so different and why it announced the arrival of modern painting. He used to say that painting was like thinking with your brush."

"I understand it better now. Monet looked with his eyes, Van Gogh with his heart, and Cézanne with his mind."

"I guess you could say that, yes."

"This Mona Lisa is pretty. She's covered in little dots!"

"This is a painting by Georges Seurat."

"Did he have dots in his head, just like Van Gogh had waves in his?"

"In order to draw all these thousands of little dots you'd have to be a calmer person, not someone as tormented as Van Gogh, don't you think?"

"But, then why did he draw all those dots?"

"He got this idea from Eugène Chevreul, a physician who discovered that two colors put side by side created a new shade between them that looks like a different, third color."

"It's not very easy to see that here!"

"You can only really see it on the big paintings, the ones in the museums. And anyway, it's always better to see paintings in real life. But to get back to Seurat, he was trying to find a link between art and science."

"Was he a researcher too, like Cézanne?"

"I suppose so, yes. He was a researcher, but the important thing for him was that his painting be beautiful. There's another very nice Seurat painting that you must have seen before. It's called *A Sunday Afternoon on the Island of La Grande Jatte*. It shows people walking along the banks of the river Seine and a pretty lady under a parasol."

"Now this one is a Fauvist *Mona Lisa*, which means wild."

"You mean wild like a lion?"

"Yes, wild like a lion. During an exhibition, a French journalist thought that the colors used were too violent and gave this painting style the name 'Fauve,' which means 'wild beast' in French."

"But it's not that violent."

"At the time it was. It doesn't shock you because you're used to bright colors. These days they're everywhere. The most famous Fauvist painters are Henri Matisse and André Derain (1880–1954). Henri Matisse used to say, 'When I use green, it doesn't mean grass, and when I use blue, it doesn't mean the sky.'"

"He sounds like Gauguin."

"You're right. Maybe Gauguin was really the first Fauvist. It was a movement that didn't last very long though. Quite often, painters borrowed a name used by critics to make fun of them and united around it, using it to get more attention. As the saying goes, there's strength in numbers."

PICASSO

"I recognize this Mona Lisa. We have the same one at school, with the eye in the middle of her face!"

"So, you know who painted it?"

"Picasso!"

"Yes, Pablo Picasso, a Spanish painter who lived in France. And do you know why her eye is in the middle of her face?"

"No. "

"Look carefully at her face. Is it a frontal view or is it in profile?"

"In profile."

"Are you sure?"

"Yes."

"Are the eyes, nostrils, and mouth all in profile too?"

"Ah no! They're facing us!"

"Picasso painted a profile that looks right at us at the same time. You could say he knew how to turn heads."

"The landscape in the background is like Cézanne's squares."

"That's right. When he was a young man, Picasso and his painter friend Georges Braque (1882–1963) went to a big exhibition of Cézanne's work in Paris. When they came out they were extremely excited:

PICASSO: Well?
BRAQUE: It's crazy how he paints his different planes.
PICASSO: We could do better than that though.
BRAQUE: You mean, show all sides at once?
PICASSO: Yes, as if you were walking around a cube.
BRAQUE: Shall we go to your workshop or mine?
PICASSO: Let's go to mine!"

"Were you there, Dad?"

"No, I'm just imagining what they said. That's how these two great painters, inspired by Cézanne's work, tried to go one step further and show all sides of the image at once. Just as if they were turning a cube round and round, looking at each of its sides. That's why they came to be known as Cubists. I could tell you a lot more about Picasso, one of the twentieth century's greatest painters, but we have to move on . . ."

"Was he better than Leonardo da Vinci?"

"You can't compare them, because they didn't live in the same time period. But just like Leonardo da Vinci knew how to capture life in a face, Picasso knew how to capture it in bodies."

"What is his most famous painting?"

"It's called *Les Demoiselles d'Avignon*."

"This one has a moustache! And why are there letters underneath it?"

"Read them out loud."

"L . . . H . . . O . . . O . . . Q . . . I don't understand!"

"It was the French artist Marcel Duchamp who drew the moustache on the *Mona Lisa* just after the 1914 war. If a French person read those letters like you just did, they would hear a rude word."

"Why did he do that?"

"The First World War, which killed millions of people, had just finished. As a reaction to its barbarity, several artists formed an art movement that they called Dada."

"That's a baby word . . ."

"Exactly. They wanted to promote the spirit of childhood and mockery. If art and culture weren't able to stop such horrific things, like war, from happening, then art and culture must be worthless. And if that is true, then all you can do is laugh."

"And so they drew a moustache on the *Mona Lisa*?"

"Yes, and on culture and art as a whole. Duchamp wrote: 'After all these millions of deaths, let's invent the smile of tomorrow.' He wasn't officially part of the Dada movement, but he was with them in spirit. As you'll see, he was like an artistic movement all on his own. He shook the art world by completely changing how we view creativity. Duchamp's real name was Villon. Do you know why he chose to use this fake name, which was actually his mother's name?"

"No."

"Because in French, the expression 'prendre du champ' means to step backwards, to look elsewhere. He created a concept that he called 'Readymade.' For example, Duchamp took a stool and attached a bike wheel to it. That's a Readymade."

"So a Readymade is when you don't actually 'make' anything at all?"

"You've got it! You don't do anything—or perhaps just something small like adding a wheel to a stool."

"But that's not art!"

"Duchamp didn't want to make art anymore. He hated the word 'artist.'"

"Why? Why didn't he want to be an artist?"

"It could have been because he was upset at the bad reception he got for one of his pieces, *Nude Descending a Staircase*. He must have thought to himself: 'They're all dumb. I'll show them what art really is.' To help you understand his thinking, I'll tell you about one of his most famous Readymades. Duchamp exhibited an upside-down urinal that he called *Fountain*, signed by the manufacturer R. Mut and presented as a work of art. Think about those four phrases. It's all back to front. The point is to make us think a little."

"So, was that the end of art and painting?"

"No, painting can't just disappear. It's been part of our story since prehistoric times. But something else had been born now and art was no longer just something retinal."

"What does retinal mean?"

"The eye, the retina. Art became a matter of pure thought. No more expert skill or the craftsmanship of a painter's work. From this point on, any artist following in Duchamp's footsteps had to be very smart."

"And funny too!"

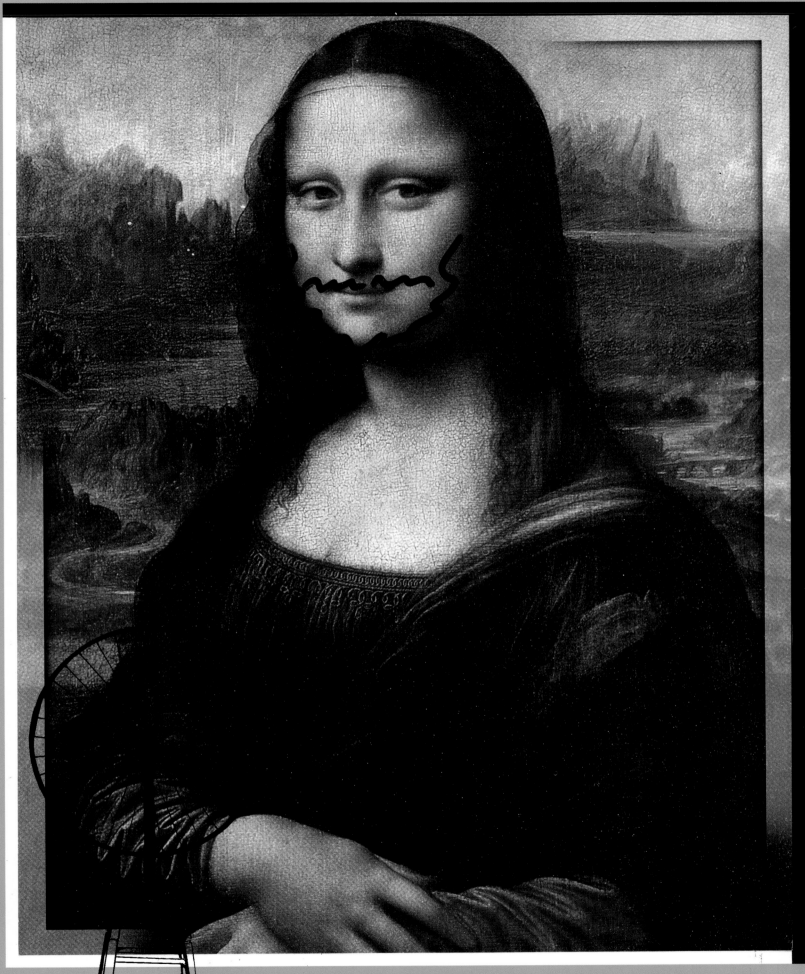

LHOOQ

MARCEL DUCHAMP (1887–1968) 19

Malevitch

"That's not the *Mona Lisa*. It's just some symbols."

"It's by the Russian painter Kazimir Malevich. He used geometric shapes to make up his pictures. In Russia, they were in the middle of a revolution. The revolution wanted to invent a new world and Malevich a new kind of painting."

"Like Picasso, with the eye in the middle of the face?"

"No, not really. Picasso had created a new kind of representation of the world, but his models were still natural. There were still faces, bodies, landscapes. As for Malevich, he painted using geometric shapes: squares, triangles, rectangles, circles, and crosses. Signs that were invented by humans. It was his way of placing man at the center of creation. Malevich called this movement Suprematism."

"Like God, the Supreme Being?"

"Yes, and just like God, he was all alone. He was pretty much the only member of his new movement."

"He must have been kind of crazy."

"You have to be a bit crazy to wander off the beaten track like that. The Russian Revolution was like a promise that finally anything was going to be possible. The artists at the time were very excited at that prospect. 'Let's just wipe the slate clean,' said the Revolutionaries. So Malevich painted a white square on a black background, like an invisible door that made everything else disappear. An empty space on which to reinvent the world."

"Duchamp drew a moustache on the *Mona Lisa* and Malevich made it disappear . . ."

"That's it! Malevich, with his signs, had invented abstract painting. Painting that has nothing to do with reality, that isn't imitating the world in any way. But his dream quickly became a nightmare as the revolutionaries turned into jailers. Malevich was imprisoned and tortured. After his release, he started painting again, but this time in a much more classical style."

"Was he scared of going back to jail?"

"I'm sure he was."

"Why did the revolutionaries turn out that way?"

"Because they wiped the slate clean."

"But so did Malevich."

"You can do anything you want with art, because it's not reality. It's like a dream, like the imagination. Anything can exist. But in real life, if you erase the past, history, culture, and everything else that makes up mankind, then you become a barbarian."

"So, in art, you can do anything you want?"

"Yes, anything. But if art becomes reality, then it is no longer art."

WASSILY Kandinsky

"This one's just a scribble . . ."

"This is the work of another Russian painter, Wassily Kandinsky. You have to look at it in the same way you would listen to music."

"You mean look with my ears?"

"Sort of, yes. This painter was very interested in harmony between colors and rhythms. Bit by bit, his scribbles become more structured, and he started to form geometric shapes. Look at the Mona Lisa herself. She is geometric, but the landscape behind is more scribbly. It makes sense to compare it to music. Kandinsky believed that there was a link between color and sound. Do you remember Seurat? He talked about colors as if they were vibrations. Sound is vibration. Maybe one day scientists will figure out how to bring sound and color together."

"So, one day we could listen to Kandinsky's music you mean?"

"Maybe one day, yes."

"Did Malevich want to make music too?"

"No, Malevich mostly used black and white, whereas Kandinsky's paintings were very colorful."

"But is it also abstract painting?"

"Yes. The story goes that once Kandinsky found one of his paintings upside down in the corner of his studio, and he was struck at the harmony between the colors. The painting was of some Russian peasant women, wearing colorful dresses against a snowy background."

"Are there other abstract painters?"

"Of course. There is one in particular that I know you will like; a Dutchman called Mondrian who inspired the French fashion designer Yves Saint Laurent to create one of his dresses."

"Is fashion art as well?"

"It is when it's Yves Saint Laurent."

WASSILY KANDINSKY (1866–1944)   23

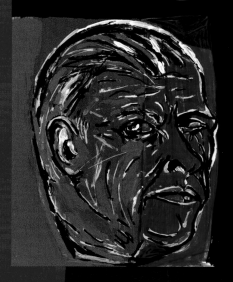

"This one is scary."

"This is an expressionist *Mona Lisa* by the German painter Otto Dix."

"It makes me think of death."

"The painting expresses what a lot of artists felt when confronted with the horrors of war—past and future—that surrounded them. One of the first expressionist works of art was *The Scream* by the Norwegian painter Edvard Munch (1893). As he was crossing a bridge one evening, the sunset lit up the sky and everything looked as though it were drenched in blood. Munch began to tremble and felt as though an infinite scream were slicing through the entire universe. *The Scream* is the very definition of Expressionism."

"I wouldn't like to have that on my bedroom wall. I don't think I could sleep."

"It was made to keep you awake."

HaïM SOUTINE

"This one's making a silly face. She must be an expressionist Mona Lisa too."

"You're starting to develop a good eye!"

"It's easy. If she's making a face or looks scary then it must be expressionist."

"Yes, but Soutine didn't paint violent scenes like the German Expressionists. He painted bouquets of flowers, landscapes, and ordinary people instead. There's one kind of expressionism in the way you choose your subject and another in the way you put the painting on the canvas. Haïm Soutine, who painted this Mona Lisa, had a style that nobody in France had ever seen before."

"Was he French?"

"No, he was Russian and was one of hundreds of other artists—from Poland, Romania, Hungary—who went to France to study art in Paris. Paris, with all of its museums and academies, was like a school for them. That's why we call them the School of Paris painters."

"It doesn't look like Soutine learned much to me. It looks like he painted with his fingers!"

"You know, sometimes you have to look at a lot of different paintings by an artist to understand his or her world and to decide whether you like it or not. I bet that if you saw an exhibition dedicated to Soutine, you would come to like his work a lot."

"He reminds me of Van Gogh. He uses waves in a similar way. But they go in all directions, as if there's a storm. Did he have waves in his head too?"

"No, the waves in his work are a result of lessons he took as a child in Hebraic scripture, which is made up of little flecks, like baby waves."

"What does that have to do with painting?"

"Handwriting is a person's first initiation into drawing. If you learn to do something in childhood, you often tend to reproduce it later on. His artist friends from the School of Paris used waves in their paintings too. Do you know who went to his funeral? I'll give you a hint: He was a famous painter."

"Leonardo da Vinci?"

"Oh, come on!"

"Um . . . Picasso?"

"Yes, Picasso was there. He was so blown away by this primitive painting style, which was so full of life, that on that summer's day in 1943, he decided to go pay one last tribute to Haïm Soutine."

"Now here we are in Russia again. This is a constructivist *Mona Lisa*."

"Like a construction worker? Is that why she was drawn with a ruler?"

"You've got it. The Constructivists distanced themselves from pure painting. They believed that art was meant to be applied to all fields. It was the Russian Revolution, and the new citizens needed engineers and architects more than they needed artistic painters. They needed machines more than canvases."

"You're right. This Mona Lisa does kind of look like a machine."

"The person that founded this movement was called Vladimir Tatlin, a painter and sculptor who was interested in architecture. He designed a tower that was supposed to be a monument to the glory of the Russian Revolution, but at that time they hadn't developed the right techniques to build it. It remained in the planning stage forever."

"This Mona Lisa looks like a constructor."

"Constructivist, not constructor! You're right, though; this is the same movement as in Russia, only this time in Germany. This is Bauhaus, a German word that means 'building house' and that brings together all the different kinds of artists: craftsmen, engineers, architects, visual artists. The Bauhaus artists believed, just like the Constructivists, that art shouldn't just be about creation, but should also serve society in some way: 'The end goal of any visual activity is construction . . . together we will create the construction of the future, which will embrace architecture, visual arts, and painting in one single form.' Many of the objects and furniture that surround us today were created under this same influence. What we call design today was thought up by the Bauhaus artists. Bauhaus came to an end in 1933 though, when it was closed down once and for all under the Nazi oppression."

"I like this Mona Lisa. She kind of looks like a dream!"

"This is a surrealist *Mona Lisa*. Surrealism was a follow-up to Dada, which was shooting off in all directions. The poet André Breton decided to organize this new movement by publishing a manifesto in 1924: Surrealism proposes to express—verbally, by means of the written word, or in any other manner—the actual functioning of thought in the absence of any control exercised by reason. He also inspired the dream analysis of the great psychoanalyst Sigmund Freud."

"Did he want to paint dreams?"

"The dreams and subconscious thoughts that are buried deep inside us. The most famous painters of this movement were the Belgian artist René Magritte and, even more so, Salvador Dali, who was from Spain."

"The one with the upturned moustache?"

"Yes, the one whose moustache pointed towards the sky. If you want, I can teach you a surrealist game. You get a piece of paper and write down any word that comes into your head. You fold the paper to hide what you have written. You pass the paper to your friend, who does the same thing and then passes it to someone else, and so on until it gets to the last person, who opens and reads it. This game is called 'cadavre exquis,' which literally means 'exquisite corpse,' because the first time the Surrealists played it the sentence read: The exquisite corpse will drink the new wine."

"But what's the point?"

"It's a sentence that doesn't bother with the laws of logic, just like dreams. It's a free, surrealist poem."

"You can see the landscape in the background through her face."

"This is a *Mona Lisa* by Francis Picabia, an artist famous for his transparencies, just like you said. Here, the various planes are all jumbled together. I could have told you all about the history of painting, from the Impressionists to today, just by using Picabia's work. He did everything."

"Even Readymades?"

"Yes, even Readymades. He was a good friend of Duchamp, who he met in New York in 1915. They had lots of fun together. But whereas Duchamp lived quite a simple life, Picabia lived like a prince."

"Was he rich?"

"Yes. It's because of this—and his talent, too, of course—that he was able to be so productive."

"Is money important?"

"It's very important. I could also tell you the whole history of art through just his financial backers and art dealers. The Viennese writer Stefan Zweig said that nobody knew painting better than art dealers."

"Why not?"

"When you bet your fortune on an unknown artist, it's important that you don't make a mistake. There is no such thing as a great painting movement without great art dealers. Paul Durand-Ruel for the Impressionists; Daniel-Henry Kahnweiler for the Cubists; Léo Castelli for Pop-art; and Charles Saatchi for today's young English scene, one of the most creative current movements."

"Did Leonardo da Vinci have financial backers?"

"No, he had people who commissioned work from him: the king, princes, the Church. In 2007, an English artist named Damien Hirst produced a piece that consisted of a laughing skull covered in 8,601 diamonds. He put it up for sale at $74 million and became the richest living artist in the world."

"So, if something's expensive, does that make it good?"

"These days there is a lot of confusion between market value and artistic value. Damien Hirst enjoys playing around with this confusion."

"Has he earned a lot of money?"

"Oh yes!"

"Ew! This one's ugly! Are we going to see some nice ones again soon?"

"But this one is nice! It's a *Mona Lisa* by Francis Bacon, an Irish painter who was a big fan of Picasso. But whereas Picasso shows the exuberance of life, Francis Bacon's work is violent and dark."

"If he was inspired by Picasso, why did he draw such sad pictures?"

"We paint what we are. Bacon didn't paint violent scenes in the same way the Expressionists did, but he expressed his own violence through his painting style."

"What about the lines all over the face?"

"They are mostly curves that he used to distort the face without it becoming just one big smudge. He often displayed his subjects in geometric frames, like transparent prisons in which the bodies were held captive. He was actually expressing his own feelings of oppression and suffering."

"It looks like he paints with his fingers, like Soutine."

"His fingers, his brush, and also tubes of paint, which he would crush against the canvas. It's almost as if Bacon painted with a knife or a scalpel. The face of this Mona Lisa looks as though the flesh has been cut out, like a stencil. He always liked to quote this line by the poet Aeschylus: 'The smell of blood is always with me.'"

"I never want to go see a Francis Bacon exhibition."

"Maybe when you're older. Bacon wasn't trying to create horror, just paint it. Right down to its most visceral representations. As if he were pulling out people's hearts to grab hold of life itself."

"Was he a serial killer?"

"No, he must have been a very good man, but he suffered a lot on the inside. You can see that just by looking at his paintings. That's what they embody."

"What does 'embody' mean?"

"It means using the body to show life. Leonardo da Vinci, Van Gogh, Picasso, Soutine, Bacon—they were all trying to do that in their work. It's the hardest part, but when you get it right, it becomes something universal and timeless."

"Like the *Mona Lisa*'s smile?"

"Exactly, like the *Mona Lisa*'s smile. It's what every painting aims to do. Painters have a different way of looking at things, but they're all looking for beauty. They see it where others don't. For them, good taste and bad taste are barriers that don't exist."

America after 1945

1945

WILLEM De KOONING

"I feel like I've seen this *Mona Lisa* before."

"This one is by Willem de Kooning, another painter who admired Picasso."

"They all admired Picasso."

"That's because he was the best."

"This one looks kind of scribbled. She's scary too—a bit like the expressionist paintings."

"You're really learning how to look now. But instead of saying 'scribbled,' what's the more technical word that would fit here?"

"Abstract."

"Exactly. This movement became known as Abstract Expressionism."

"That was easy!"

36   WILLEM DE KOONING (1904–1997)

"Let's leave France now and fly to the United States."

"The United States?"

"Yes, to 1945, the end of the Second World War. The Americans were victorious and the country was young and powerful. A lot of artists fled a devastated Europe and took refuge in New York: Duchamp, Picabia, Breton, and so forth. This mix of a young and dynamic country with the European avant-garde quickly turned the city into the art capital of the world."

"Paris wasn't the center anymore?"

"No, that part was over for Paris. In New York, everything was big: the city, the studios, the apartments. The painters could produce huge canvases. They would set them up in front of them or even lay them on the floor. No more stools and easels! Now they could actually stand in front of their work. This is what was called Action Painting. Gigantism was the primary characteristic of American painting."

"This one looks like someone dropped paint on the canvas."

"This is a Jackson Pollock *Mona Lisa*. He would lay his canvas out on the floor and paint from above. He threw paint by flicking a stick that he had dipped in different colored pots."

"Was he the first person to paint on the floor like that?"

"Not the first. He was copying the Native Americans, who painted magic on the ground using colored sand in order to communicate with the spirits of their elders, who were thought to be underground. Magic is an ancestor of religion. In our culture, religious painting looks to the sky, the place we imagine God to be. To look at frescos or stained glass you have to look up. When Pollock showed his work in a gallery, it was as if he was turning the room upside down, making the floor and walls switch places."

"Did he paint magic on the walls?"

"He tried. But he wasn't a shaman."

"What's a shaman?"

"A bit like a witch. Art hasn't always meant the same thing at different periods and for different civilizations. What we understand today by the word 'artist' is a recent, Western creation."

WARHOL

"There are lots of Mona Lisas here, and this time they're pretty!"

"These were painted by Andy Warhol, a New York artist."

"Why are they all the same?"

"Warhol was the first American artist to paint in a way that ignored all European influences. The United States was a society of consumerism and mass production. Warhol used this idea and called his studio The Factory. He used a machine to print his paintings manually, which allowed him to produce series of the same image. This process is called screen-printing. I'll draw a little diagram to help you understand."

Factory ➜ Workers ➜ Machine ➜ Products
Factory ➜ Painter ➜ Screen-printing ➜ Picture

"So, we're not really talking about painting anymore?"

"It is still like painting, because when he printed his photos onto the canvas, he did them one after another, causing the images to fade bit by bit. This meant that each Mona Lisa was slightly different. After that, he colored them. He printed Mona Lisas, Coke bottles, Campbell soup cans, and movie stars like Marilyn Monroe."

"He put cans in his paintings as though they were art?"

"Yes, and the Mona Lisa as though she was a consumer product. By printing his photos like this, he was working in a similar way to Marcel Duchamp. He was producing Readymades. His work was different from Duchamp's though, because it was mass-produced."

"I don't really understand."

"Duchamp believed that the act of repeating something, starting the same thing over again, created taste."

"Taste?"

"Seeing something over and over again is what makes you decide whether you think it's beautiful or ugly; it's called aesthetics. Duchamp didn't want his Readymades to become aesthetic objects or works of art. He deliberately limited the number he produced. They were there to provoke thought and nothing else. Warhol did the same thing as Duchamp but in mass-production. In this way, he created a new kind of aesthetic."

"How did he come up with the idea of painting Campbell's soup cans?"

"He loved this brand of soup. Once he was eating with his mom . . ."

"He lived with his mom?"

"Yes. So, during lunch, he asked her:

WARHOL: **Mom, what do you think I should paint?**
HIS MOM: **Paint these soup cans, Andrew, you know how much you love this soup.**

She was getting a bit tired of all the questions her eccentric son would ask her. Andy Warhol got up and quickly left the table.

HIS MOM: **Aren't you going to finish your soup, Andrew?**
WARHOL: **No, I'm going to paint it.**
HIS MOM: **Don't forget to call if you'll be home late!**
WARHOL: **Yes, Mom.**

For Andy Warhol, fame was the very definition of beauty. And because America had so many stars and famous products, he decided to put them down on his canvas. By treating popular icons as works of art, he became one of the major figures of what would become known as Pop-art."

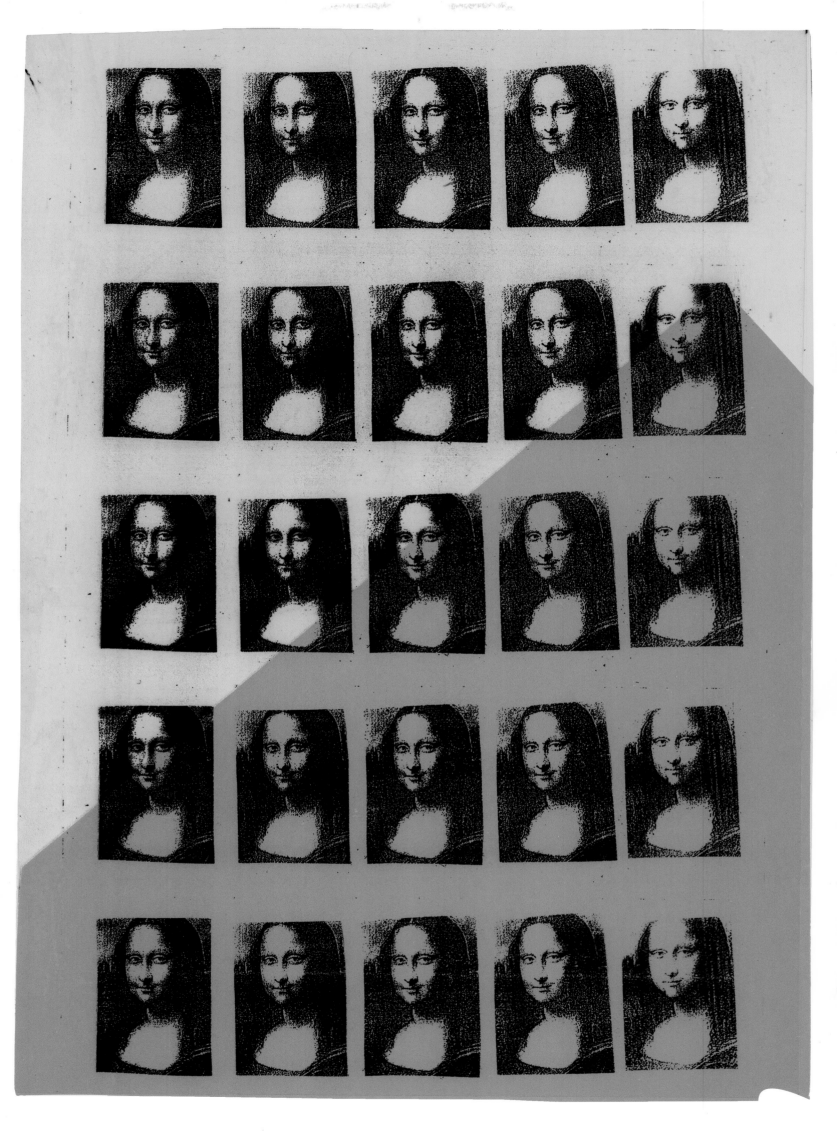

ROY LICHTENSTEIN

"This one looks like a cartoon."

"Yes, the painting process is similar to that of cartoons, with black outlines filled in with bright colors. This *Mona Lisa* is by Roy Lichtenstein, an American painter. Like Warhol, he reproduced magazine images onto his canvases, but he actually painted them by hand. The tiny dots that you see are like a blown up version of a printed image."

"Is he a Pop-artist too?"

"Yes. It was his son who gave him the idea. His son was reading Mickey Mouse one day and asked his dad whether he was that good at drawing too. That's how Lichtenstein began reproducing magazine images."

"This one makes my eyes hurt!"

"This is an Op art *Mona Lisa*."

"Op?"

"It comes from the word optical. It's art that uses optical illusions."

"Like Seurat with all his little dots?"

"Yes, I suppose you could say that Seurat was the first person to take new notions of perception and apply them to his art. He wasn't trying to create visual confusion though—quite the opposite in fact—but that is exactly what the op art artists were trying to do. Victor Vasarely, a French artist born in Hungary, was a key figure in this movement."

"Why did they want to cause visual confusion?"

"To ask questions. Think of a fly, or maybe a cat; they have a different kind of vision than we do. Maybe the world you see is just an illusion."

"Let's go back to France."

"I thought we were done with France."

"In the 1960s, a French art critic named Pierre Restany brought together several artists and elaborated on his theory of New Realism. It was a way of resisting the power of America."

"This *Mona Lisa* is all ripped up though."

"This is by Jacques Villeglé, what we call a found-object artist. He would walk around the streets collecting old bits of posters. There are lots of layers, old ones under new ones, and he saw these as being like layers of time. Another artist, sculptor Pierre Arman, piled cars on top of each other and embedded them in concrete. He could compile all sorts of things like watches, glasses, and so on. Another of his friends, Cesar, who was also a sculptor, compressed cars into cube shapes."

"Weren't there any painters?"

"Yes, Yves Klein, for example. He lived in Nice, by the sea in the south of France. He loved the blue of the sky so much that if a seagull flew across it, it made him really angry. He thought that the white line polluted the sky. So, he set about doing paintings that were entirely blue."

"Just blue, on its own?"

"Yes, we call it monochrome—just one color."

"Everything Malevich did was white."

"He lived in Russia, where everything is white in the winter. Yves Klein invented a blue that he called IKB (International Klein Blue), like a brand name for an industrial product. To get back to Restany's definition, New Realism is a poetic recycling of urban, industrial, and advertising reality."

"So, did they manage to beat the Americans?"

"No, but they did get some international acclaim, and Arman became a very important sculptor. And he moved to the United States."

"Was it hard if you didn't live in America?"

"Well, where does Superman live?"

"In America!"

"This *Mona Lisa* is just an outline. There isn't anything there!"

"This is a piece of minimalist art by the artist Joseph Kosuth. Minimalism was a movement that was a reaction to Abstract Expressionism and to the abundance of brightly colored images being created by the pop artists."

"Why do they always want to do the opposite?"

"It's a way of moving forward, of searching, existing, making yourself known."

"Like trying to be fashionable?"

"If you like, yes. The Minimalists made no distinction between the object on display and the space in which it was displayed. Those were the two things that made up the work of art."

"I don't get it."

"Let's make up an example of a minimalist work of art. On top of the floorboards, going in the same direction, I build a rectangle and fill it with water. Everything will be reflected in it. I'm changing the perception you have of the floor and of the room. The work shows the place, and the place shows the work."

"Can you give me another example?"

"You can do the same thing with light and with structures. Minimalism is one of the important origins of modern sculpture and conceptual art."

"Conceptual?"

"Conceptual art, in broad terms, can be described as an idea. Look at this Mona Lisa."

"But it's not a *Mona Lisa*. It's a word!"

"Yes, the word 'smile.' And so the *Mona Lisa* is . . . ?"

"She's smiling."

"When you write the word 'smile' on a canvas, it's like you're creating a conceptual *Mona Lisa*."

"It's easier to understand than painting. So, Dad, what is 'laugh' the concept of?"

"I don't know."

"It's The Laughing Cow!"

"Not bad!"

MINIMALISM—JOSEPH KOSUTH (1945–)   45

Gerhard Richter

"This Mona Lisa is blurry, but I still think she's pretty!"

"This is a German painter, Gerhard Richter. He paints most of all from images, magazine photos, and newspapers. By blurring the photos, he jumbles up their message."

"What message?"

"What the images were trying to say to us."

"What's the difference between an image and a painting?"

"Images explain or sell things. They are a tool that promotes a person or a product. They are aimed at as many people as possible. A painting, though, acts from the inside. It's more intimate; it only speaks about itself. And everyone who looks at it sees something different. It's the opposite with an image, where everyone is supposed to see and understand the same thing. The message is: 'Vote for me, buy me.'"

"Do you prefer paintings or images?"

"I don't look at them in the same way. As I just said, images and paintings have different functions, but sometimes the borders between them are a little blurred. Gerhard Richter uses this blurring to shake up the intention behind an image and turn it into a painting. This isn't the only kind of painting he does though; he also paints abstract and figurative works of art. Painting is all he needs in life; everything else is just words."

"What do you think of this *Mona Lisa*?"

"It's not like the others."

"This one is by Jean-Michel Basquiat, a young American who started by painting walls in the street. It's what became known later as street art, or urban art."

"But he wasn't allowed to do that!"

"He did it anyway. If you look carefully at his paintings there are streets, cars, housing blocks, and roads at right angles. It's New York, his city. Basquiat was a musician. His pieces are like a kind of strange sheet music. If you want to listen to the music of New York, you just have to look at one of Jean-Michel Basquiat's paintings."

"What kind of music was it?"

"All genres of African American music, except maybe disco. Basquiat was the first major African American artist to become famous internationally."

"There were no African Americans in big positions before?"

"Today we have an African American president in the United States, Barack Obama, but not too long ago this would have been unimaginable. Almost like science fiction."

"How did Basquiat become such a big painter?"

"Thanks to his talent, first of all, but also thanks to one particular meeting. When he was selling his drawings in a restaurant one day, he bumped into Andy Warhol, who bought them all. The two developed a great friendship and had a lot of admiration for each other. They even did some paintings together. Warhol was convinced that this young man was going to become the biggest artist of his day. He was proud to pass the torch down to him. Unfortunately, Basquiat died of a drug overdose at the age of just twenty-seven."

"Like a rock star?"

"Exactly. Basquiat was one of painting's first stars. He was young, handsome, and famous."

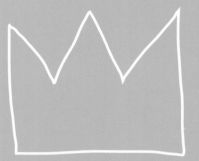

KEITH HARING

"This *Mona Lisa* was drawn by Keith Haring, who also got his start as a graffiti artist."

"Like Basquiat?"

"Yes, they were great friends. They met at Club 57, a night club that was a meeting place for the young artists on the New York scene. Musicians, painters, and so forth. Like Basquiat though, he died very young."

"Because of drugs?"

"No, he died of AIDS. Today, if you look around the walls of our city, you can see graffiti and tags. Some of these artists, the best ones, will move from city walls to art galleries and onto fame and celebrity."

French artist who writes funny sentences on canvases. For example: Nothing to say, It's just art . . ."

"One of my friends had a pencil case with one of Ben's sentences on it . . ."

"Which one?"

"I've forgotten."

"'I've forgotten?'"

"No, I mean I've forgotten!"

"Oh, I see! 'I mean I've forgotten?'"

"No!"

"Because of these sentences, which we see everywhere and recognize by their graphics, Ben has become a brand, like Adidas or Nike. By poking fun at art, artists' egos, and the art market, he actually tells us a lot about our current time and all of its vanities."

"What's an ego?"

"The ego is the 'me, I'; the ridiculous side of many of today's artists."

"What about you, Dad? Are you ridiculous too?"

"I hope so!"

"I like this *Mona Lisa* a lot! It's like a box of colored pencils."

"You're right; it makes you think of childhood. This is by Robert Combas, a French painter who is inspired by popular imagery: cartoons, signs, kids' drawings. Behind a figurative appearance hides an abstract painting. Looking back, I think that all I do is abstract paintings, but then I add flowers, a house, Dad, Mom, everything that reminds me of my childhood. Combas belonged to the movement called Free Figuration, which was given its name by Ben, a

"This is an Internet *Mona Lisa*."

"I see lots of little squares."

"Those are what we call digital pixels. It's a *Mona Lisa* done on the computer. This marked the beginning of the future. Leonardo da Vinci was around when the printing press was starting its life, a discovery that was just as important then as the Internet is today. We are in the midst of a new Renaissance. An artist in Africa can talk to an artist in New York City, who in turn can communicate with an artist in China. Borders are disappearing. Globalization and instant communication are shaking up the art world. The network and the web have become a canvas for artists. The art market will be greatly changed by this invention. You just have to look at music, for example, and see what a huge impact digital downloads have had on the CD market."

"I love this Mona Lisa. She shines in the dark!"

"This one's by a French artist called Piotr Barsony, who was born in Toulouse, France."

"I think I know him!"

"You're right. I painted this one myself. It's so shiny that you can see your reflection in it."

"So, whoever is looking at it is in the painting too?"

"Yes. All he or she has to do is smile and they become the Mona Lisa too."

"How do you make it so shiny?"

"I paint on transparent polyester, mostly using a paint gun, an airbrush, or sometimes a regular brush. This technique allows me to give off a light similar to the light that comes off a television or computer screen."

"Do you like that kind of light?"

"Do you remember the song I wrote about the TV? The chorus went like this: 'Without images and without noise, like a moment of clarity, how beautiful, how beautiful a TV is.' My inspiration came from this piece of light-up furniture. All of these screens are just part of our environment these days. There are artists who make videos, others who make installations with TVs and computers. Me, I'm more interested in the surface of things. The screen and the light."

"You're like a Screen Impressionist!"

"I hadn't thought of it like that."

"I like your paintings. At night everything is reflected in them."

"Well, here we are at the end of our little trip. There are a lot of painters we couldn't talk about here; it's hard to look at everything at once. But I hope that this story has helped you learn how to think about painting."

"You mean look at painting!"

"Look, think, understand, enjoy contemplating a work of art. That's what I've tried to teach you. If not, you're like someone who doesn't know how to read, who can marvel at the calligraphy when looking at a manuscript, but is too ignorant to understand what is written. In modern art, everything is expressed; the best and the worst. That's the price of freedom. There are lots and lots of snobs out there, but also some rare artists who tell us a little something about our moment in time and who can help us better understand it. Now it's your turn to do your own research and, who knows, maybe one day I'll come into your studio to admire your work."

"I think that when I grow up, I'm going to be a singer."

"A singer?"

"Yes, because they get to wear nice dresses."

"That's a good enough reason."

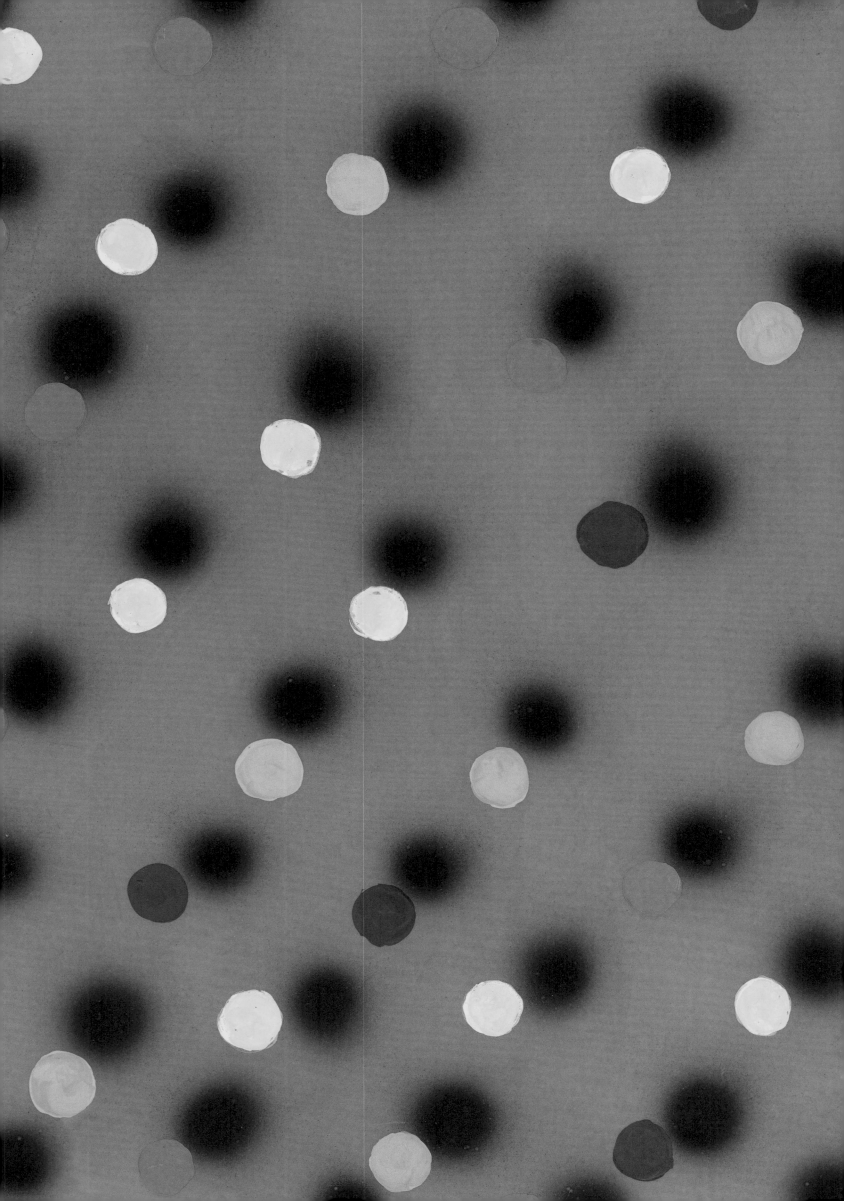